PIANO · VOCAL · GUITAR

MW01670650

TOP CHRISTIAN HITS OF '06-'07

ISBN-13: 978-1-4234-2457-4
ISBN-10: 1-4234-2457-3

HAL•LEONARD®
CORPORATION
7777 W. BLUEMOUND RD. P.O. BOX 13819 MILWAUKEE, WI 53213

ALL THAT I AM

Words and Music by MARC DODD,
MATT FUQUA, JOSHUA HAVENS
and BRAD WIGGERS

In a strong two

Recorded a half step lower.

D A/D Em/D D Bm A/B
Spir - it; it's mov - ing a - round me.
with me e - ven when I'm all a - lone.
G(add2)/B Bm D A/D Em/D D
I hear Your voice, You're call - ing me clos -
When I close my eyes, You're call - ing me clos -
Bm A/B G(add2)/B Bm D A/D
- er. I know that You're here,
- er. When I pull a - way,
Em/D D Bm A/B G(add2)/B Bm
You're call - ing me clos - er.
You're pull - ing me clos - er.
And

E7/G♯
A
D
A/C♯
I will love You with all of my heart.
f
Bm7
A
D
A/C♯
Bm7
A
Jesus, I'll love You with all of my mind. Jesus, I'll love
D
A/C♯
Bm7
A
1
D
A/C♯
You with all of my soul. Jesus, I'll love You with all that I am.
Bm7
A/C♯
D
A/D
Em/D
3fr
D
mf

Bm
A/B
G(add2)/B
Bm
2
D
A/C♯
I know that You hear___ You with all___ that I am._
Bm7
Gmaj7
F♯m/G
mf
Gmaj7
F♯m/G
D
Dmaj7
Em/D
3fr
D
Gmaj7
A/G
You___ are
Gmaj7
A/G
D
A/D
Gmaj7/D
D
ho - ly, Lord God Al - might - y.

Gmaj7 A/G Gmaj7 A/G D A/D
You ___ are ho - ly, Lord God Al -
Gmaj7/D D Gmaj7 A/G Gmaj7 A/G
might - y, who was and __ is and soon will __ come, who
Bm A/B Bm A/B Gmaj7 A/G
was and __ is and soon will __ come, who was and __ is and
Gmaj7 A/G Bm A/B Bm A/B
soon will __ come, who was and __ is and soon will __ come.

Gmaj7
D
A/D
Lord, You are, and now You'll come a - gain.
Em/D
D
Bm
A/B
Em/B
Bm
You're com - ing a - gain. Just like You
D
A/D
Em/D
D
Bm
A/B
Em/B
Bm
said, You're com - ing a - gain. And
E7
A
D
A/C♯
Bm7
A
I will love You with all of my heart. Je - sus, I'll love
f

D A/C♯ Bm7 A D A/C♯
You with all of my mind. Je - sus, I'll love You with all of my soul.
Bm7 A D A Bm7 G
Je - sus, I'll love You with all that I am. Je - sus, I'll love
D A Bm7 G D A
You with all that I am. Je - sus, I'll love You with all that I am.
Bm7 Gmaj7 A/G D

ALL TO YOU

Words and Music by LINCOLN BREWSTER
and REID McNULTY

Moderate Shuffle

E
B
C♯m7
A
4fr
no, no.
no, no.
I've searched and
B
E
E9
came up emp - ty; this world has noth - ing for me.
A
Am
You are my one and on - ly.
E
B
C♯m7
A
4fr
I'm liv - ing my life for You,

E B C#m7 A
and I'm giv - ing ev - 'ry - thing to You.
E B/D# C#m7 B A
Not hold - ing back, but ev - 'ry part, I'm
1
F#m7 E B C#m7 A
giv - ing it all to You.
E B C#m7 A
2
F#m7
giv - ing it all to You.
4fr

E B C♯m7 A
4fr
I'm liv - ing my life for You,
E B C♯m7 A
4fr
and I'm giv - ing ev - 'ry - thing to You.
E B/D♯ C♯m7 B
4fr 4fr
Not hold - ing back, but ev - 'ry part,
A F♯m7 B C♯m7 E5
To Coda
4fr
I'm giv - ing it all to You.

F♯7
B
C♯m7
E5
I'm giv-ing it all.
(Guitar solo)
F♯7
B
C♯m7
E5
1
F♯7
B
2
F♯7
B
C♯m7
F♯7
C♯m7
F♯7

E B C♯m7 A E B
I'm liv - ing my life for You, and I'm giv - ing
C♯m7 A E B/D♯ C♯m7 B
ev - 'ry - thing to You. Not hold - ing back, but ev - 'ry part,
A F♯m7
N.C.
D.S. al Coda
I'm giv - ing it all to You.
CODA
F♯m7 E B
giv - ing it all to You.

C♯m7
A
E
B
I'm giv-ing it all to You.
(Vocal ad lib on repeat)
C♯m7
A
E
B
I'm giv-ing it all to You.
C♯m7
A
E
B
I'm giv-ing it all to You.
1
C♯m7
A
Whoa, oh.
2
C♯m7
A(add9)

ALL WHO ARE THIRSTY

Words and Music by BRENTON BROWN
and GLENN ROBERTSON

C
Am
G/B
- tain, dip your heart in the stream of
C
G
life. Let the pain and the sor - row be washed a -
Bm7
C
- way in the waves of His mer - cy.
Am
G/B
C
As the deep cries out to deep, we sing:

G
C(add2)
Come, Lord Je - sus, come.
G
Come, Lord Je - sus,
C(add2)
come.
G
Come, Lord
C(add2)
Je - sus, come.

G
C(add2)
Come, Lord Je - sus, come.
1
2
All who are thirst -
G
Won't You come?
Bm7
Won't You
C(add2)
come?
Am7
G/B
Noth - ing but Your will for me,

C
G
I am on - ly free when You come.
Bm7
C
Am7
G/B
C
Noth - ing but Your will for me, I am on - ly free when You
G
C
Come, Lord Je - sus, come.
come.
(Noth- ing but Your will for me,

G
Come, Lord Je - sus,
I am on - ly free when You...)
C
G
come.
(Noth - ing but Your will for me, I am on - ly free when You...)
Come, Lord
C
Je - sus,
come.
(Noth - ing but Your will for me, I am on - ly free when You...)
G
C(add2)
G
Come, Lord Je - sus, come.

BECAUSE OF YOUR LOVE

Words and Music by PAUL BALOCHE
and BRENTON BROWN

G/B Csus2 D G
mem - ber ev - 'ry bless - ing that You've
G/B Csus2 D G/B
poured out so free - ly from a - bove.
Csus2 G/B Csus2 D
Lift - ing grat - i - tude and prais -
G G/B Csus2 D
- es for com - pas - sion, so a - maz -

G G/B Csus2 D
- ing. Lord, we've come to give You thanks
G/B Csus2
for all You've done.
G/B Csus2 Dsus
Be-cause of Your love, we're for-giv -
G/B Csus2 Dsus G/B Csus2 Dsus
- en. Be-cause of Your love,

G/B
Csus2
Dsus
our hearts are clean.
We lift You up
G/B
Csus2
Dsus
G/B
Csus2
Dsus
with songs of free - dom.
A7/C♯
Csus2
To Coda
For - ev - er we're changed
D
G5
3fr
D.S. al Coda
(take 2nd ending)
be-cause of Your love.

CODA
D
Em7
D/F#
G
Csus2
be-cause of Your love.
(Guitar solo)
G/B
Csus2
D
Em7
D/F#
G
Csus2
G/B
Csus2
D5
5fr
G/B
Csus2
Dsus
Be-cause of Your love,
we're for-giv-

G/B Csus2 Dsus G/B Csus2 Dsus
- en. Be - cause of Your love,
G/B Csus2 Dsus
our hearts are clean. We lift You up
G/B Csus2 Dsus G/B Csus2 Dsus
with songs of free - dom.
A7/C♯ C D
For - ev - er we're changed be - cause of Your

G/B
Csus2
D
N.C.
love.
G
G/B
Csus2
D
G
Yeah.
G/B
Csus2
D
G
G/B
Csus2
D
Yeah,
yeah.
1, 2
G
3
G

GOODBYE

Words and Music by MARK STUART, WILL McGINNISS, BOB HERDMAN, TYLER BURKUM and BEN CISSELL

A/C#
D
You know I'll al - ways love you, you
A
Esus
A
know I al - ways will.
Good - bye, good - bye, good - bye,
D
my old friend.
A
E
D
Good - bye, good - bye, good - bye, we've reached the end.

A
I don't cry for sor - row, I cry with joy.
F♯m
A
The mem - o - ries we've made
F♯m
E
D
can't be de - stroyed.
You know I won't for - get
A
E
you, you know I nev - er could.
And

F♯m D A
when I said I loved you, you know I meant for good.
E A
Good-bye, good-bye, good-bye, my old friend.
D E F♯m7
Good-bye, good-bye, good-bye,
E D
we've reached the end. You know I'll al - ways love

E
A
Dsus2
E
A
you.
D
E
F♯m7
D
Good - bye.
E
F♯m7
A/D
A
Good - bye.
Good - bye, good - bye, good - bye.
E
F♯m
D
Good - bye, good - bye, good - bye.

F♯m
D
Good - bye, good - bye, good - bye.
Good - bye, good - bye, good - bye.
cresc.
B
F♯
f
E
B
F♯
Good - bye, good - bye, good - bye,
my old friend.
E
F♯
B
Good - bye, good - bye, good - bye,

F♯
G♯m
we've reached the end.
You
E
know I won't for - get you,
you
B
F♯
G♯m
know I nev - er could.
And when I said I loved
E
B
F♯
you,
you know I meant for good.
rit.

HOLD FAST

Words and Music by BART MILLARD, BARRY GRAUL,
JIM BRYSON, NATHAN COCHRAN,
MIKE SCHEUCHZER and ROBBY SHAFFER

Gm7
E♭
3fr
to all the un - de - serv - ing;
Will we see the sun at last,
Gm7
E♭
that should cov - er all of us.
or could this be our lot in life?
F
Gm7
F
Please do not let go.
Please do not let go.
I prom - ise there is hope.
I prom - ise you there's hope.
E♭
B♭
Hold fast, help is on the way.
cresc.
f

E♭
Gm7
Hold fast,
He's come to save
the day.
B♭/D
What I've learned in my life:
one thing great-er than my strife is
His grasp.
Your grasp.
1
F
So hold fast.
Gm
E♭maj7
Gm
3fr

2
E♭maj7
F
E♭
So hold fast.
dim.
F6/9
Gm7
F/A
Cm9
You
E♭maj7
F6
may think you're all alone, and there's no way that an - y - one could know
Gm7
F/A
Cm9
what you're go - ing through. But if

E♭maj7
3fr
F6
you only hear one thing, just un - der - stand that we are all the same,
Gm7
F/A
Cm9
searching for the truth,
the truth
cresc.
E♭maj7
3fr
F6
of what we're soon to face un - less some - one comes to take our place.
f
Gm7
F/A
Cm9
Is there an - y - one?
All

E♭maj7
3fr
F6
we want is to be free,
free from our captiv - i - ty,
Lord.
Gm7
F/A
Cm9
Here He comes.
Hold
B♭
E♭
3fr
fast,
help is on the way.
Hold fast,
Gm7
E♭
3fr
He's come to save the day.
What I've learned

B♭/D
1
E♭
3fr
in my life: the one thing strong - er than my strife is Your grasp.
F
So hold
2
E♭
3fr
great - er than my strife
B♭/F
F
Gm7
is Your grasp.
So hold fast.

MY GENERATION

Words and Music by TIM NEUFELD,
JON NEUFELD, DOUG McKELVEY
and SHAUN HUBERTS

Heavy Rock

Asus2 Cmaj7 E5 Cmaj7 Asus2 Cmaj7
know there's some-thing more. Our soul has got a hole. We know, but what's it wait-ing
E5 Cmaj7 Asus2 Cmaj7 E5 Cmaj7
for? Scat-tered in the street like
Asus2 Cmaj7 E5 Cmaj7 Asus2 Cmaj7
dreams and gas-o-line, the things we wan-na be are scat-tered in the street. And
E5 Cmaj7 Asus2 Cmaj7 E5 Cmaj7
if we're com-ing clean, we seem to know we're in-com-plete.

Asus2
Cmaj7
E
Am
How do we feel?
How do we feel?
My
E
C
D
E
generation is aching for real.
Dying for love,
To Coda
Am
E
C
D
crying for truth,
my generation is aching for You.
E/G♯
A5
5fr
E5/B
C
C(♯4)
4fr

E/G♯
A5
E5/B
C
C(♯4)
A
E5
Cmaj7
Asus2
coun - try of our own is all we're ask - ing for. A place to call our home, a
coun - try of our own. We know it must be close; our souls are search - ing thru the
mf
cold, the cold, the cold.
D.S. al Coda
CODA
D
- ing for You.

E5
mf
E
Am
E
Am
Ah.
f
E
Am
Ah.

E
Am
E
How do we feel?
How do we feel?
My gen - er - a - tion is ach -
C
D
E
Am
- ing for real.
Dy - ing for love,
cry - ing for truth;
my
E
1 C
D
2 C
D
gen - er - a - tion is ach - ing for You.
- ing for You.

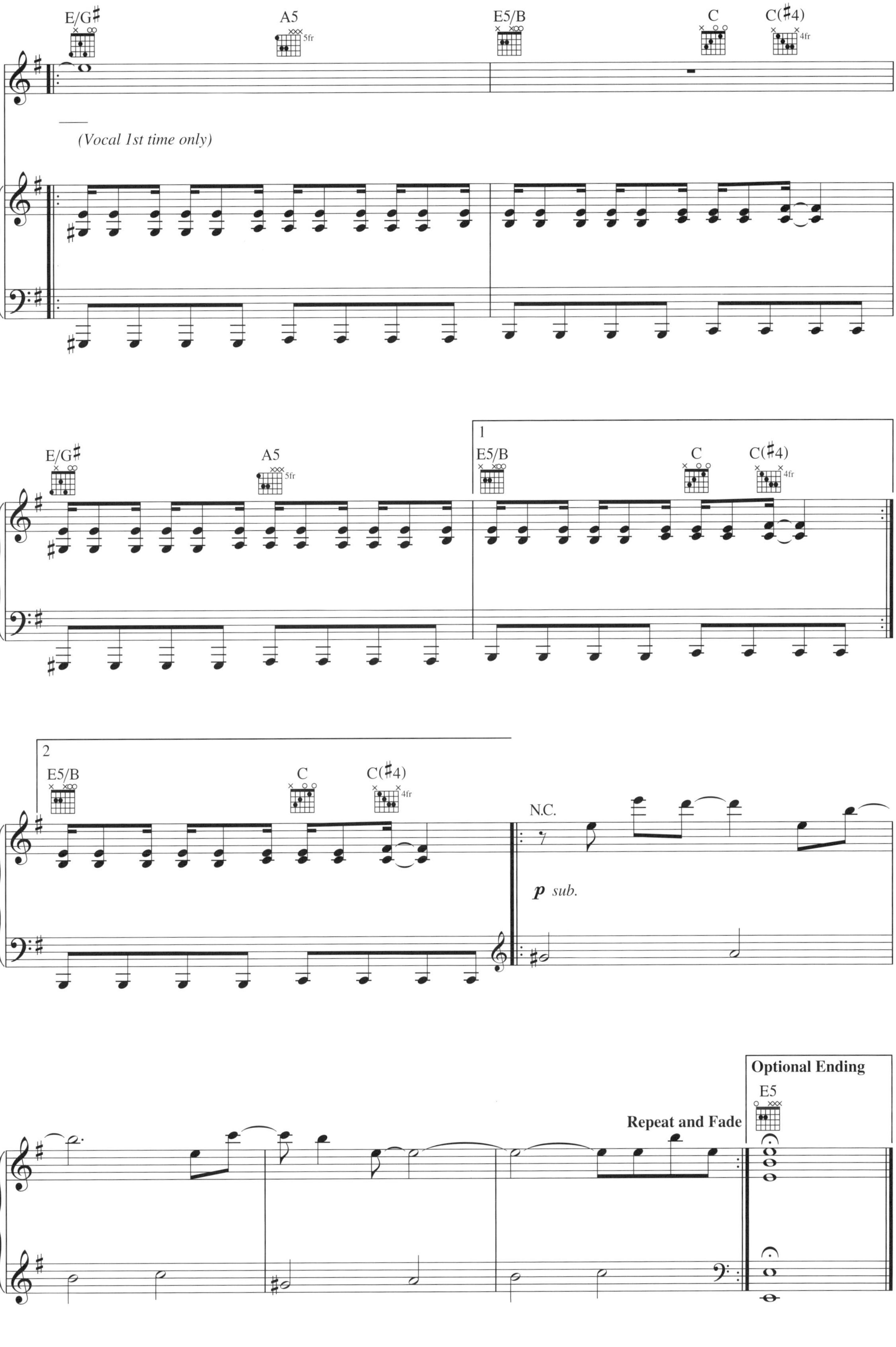
E/G♯
A5
5fr
E5/B
C
C(♯4)
4fr
(Vocal 1st time only)
1
2
N.C.
p sub.
Repeat and Fade
Optional Ending
E5

HOW GREAT IS OUR GOD

Words and Music by CHRIS TOMLIN,
JESSE REEVES and ED CASH

** Recorded a half step lower.*

Bm7
and dark - ness tries to hide. It trem - bles at His voice,
Fa - ther, Spir - it, Son, the Li - on and the Lamb,
Gmaj7
trem - bles at His voice.
Li - on and the Lamb.
How great
D
is our God! Sing with me: How great
Bm7
is our God!
Gmaj7
A
And all will see how great, how great is our God!

D
1
2
D
And
D
Bm7
Name a - bove all names, wor - thy of all praise.
Gmaj7
1
A
My heart will sing: How great is our God!
D
2
A
is our God!

D
How great is our God!
Bm7
Sing with me: How great is our God!
Gmaj7
A
And all will see how great, how great is our God!
1, 2
D
3
D
How great

LOOKING FOR YOU

Words and Music by KIRK FRANKLIN,
SHEREE BROWN, CHARLES MIMS,
PATRICE RUSHEN and FRED WASHINGTON

A♭maj7
Cm7
3fr
Fm11
6fr
I've been down so long, I've been hurt for so long,
When my en - e - mies tried to come for me,
8vb
A♭maj7
Cm7
3fr
Fm11
6fr
there were times I thought I'd nev - er see the break of day.
and they thought that my world was com - ing to an end,
8vb
A♭maj7
Cm7
3fr
Fm11
6fr
It was hard for me to see Your plan for me,
all the while You knew that I would make it through.
8vb
A♭maj7
Cm7
3fr
Fm11
6fr
and I tried to be - lieve; strug - gling won't last al - ways.
I feel clos - er to You now than when I first be - gan.
8vb

A♭maj7
Cm7
3fr
Fm11
6fr
(So night af - ter night,) night af - ter night, (night af - ter night,)
Je - sus, You are, (Je - sus, You are,) (Je - sus, You are,)
8vb
A♭maj7
Cm7
3fr
Fm11
6fr
I pray, Lord, don't take Your joy from me.
You are my sun - light af - ter the rain.
8vb
A♭maj7
Cm7
3fr
Fm11
6fr
(1.) And then late one night I read
(and then late one night)
(2., D.S.) Wher - ev - er You are I just
(wher - ev - er You are)
8vb
A♭maj7
Cm7
3fr
Fm11
6fr
in Your love let - ter that it's gon - na get bet - ter.
wan - na be near You; I'm so glad I can hear You.
Don't you know that
8vb

A♭maj7
Cm7
Fm11
3fr
6fr
I've been look - ing for You. I re - al - ize noth - ing else
will sat - is - fy me. I'm so glad I found You.
8vb
Now that I'm changed, no one can keep me a - way from You.
1
(Spoken:) You've been so good to us. You've brought us from a mighty long way.

2, 3
Fm11
6fr
A♭maj7
Cm7
3fr
That's why we love You. Come on!
keep me a - way.
I've been
8vb
look - ing for You. I re - al - ize nothing else will sat - is - fy me.
I'm so glad I found You.
To Coda
Now that I'm changed, no one can keep me a - way from You.
(Here we

Cm7
go now, here we go now, don't stop now, let's go now, in the
Cm7/F
front now, in the back now, let's go now. La - dies:)
A♭maj7 Cm7 Fm11 A♭maj7 Cm7
(Spoken:) That's for the struggle.
(Oh, oh, oh, oh, oh.) (Oh, oh,
8vb
Fm11 A♭maj7 Cm7 Fm11
That's for the pain. That's for those
oh, oh, oh.) (Oh, oh, oh, oh, oh.)
8vb
8vb

A♭maj7
Cm7
Fm11
A♭maj7
Cm7
dark nights.
(Oh, oh, oh, oh, oh.)
Je - sus, You are,
8vb
Fm11
A♭maj7
Cm7
(Je - sus, You are,) (Je - sus, You are,)
You are my sun -
8vb
Fm11
D.S. al Coda
(take 3rd ending)
- light af - ter the rain.
8vb.
CODA
Fm11
keep me a - way from You.
8vb.
A♭maj7
Cm7
Fm11
A♭maj7
Cm7
(Spoken:) So I want you to remember,
(Oh, oh, oh, oh, oh.)
no matter what happens tomorrow,
(Oh, oh,
8vb

Fm11
Abmaj7
Cm7
Fm11
Abmaj7
Cm7
6fr
3fr
God's got it all under control.
All things work together.
oh, oh, oh.)
(Oh, oh,
oh, oh, oh.)
(Oh, oh,
8vb
Fm11
Abmaj7
Cm7
Fm11
oh, oh, oh.)
Abmaj7
Cm7
Fm11
Abmaj7
Cm7
Fm11
Abmaj7
Cm7
Fm11

MADE TO WORSHIP

Words and Music by CHRIS TOMLIN,
ED CASH and STEPHAN SHARP

Moderately

C5
3fr
G/B
God on high stepped down in - to time and wrote the sto -
Brought to life. we o - pen up our eyes to see the maj -
Am7
Fsus2
Gsus
3fr
- ry of His love for ev - 'ry - one.
- es - ty and glo - ry of the King.
F
G
F
He has filled our hearts with won - der so that we al -
G
F
C
ways re - mem - ber: You and I were made to wor - ship,

Fmaj7
Dm7
you and I are called to love,
you and I are for-giv-en and free.
G
C
When you and I em-brace sur-ren-der,
Fmaj7
Dm7
G
To Coda
you and I choose to be-lieve, then you and I will see who we were meant to be.
1
C5
3fr

2
Dm7
C/E
And e-ven the rocks cry out, and e-ven the heav-ens shout
F
G
at the sound of His ho-ly name.
Dm7
C/E
So let ev-'ry voice sing out, and let ev-'ry knee bow down;
F
G
He is wor-thy of all our praise.

C
Fmaj7
You and I were made to wor - ship, you and I are called to love,
Dm7
G
C
you and I are for-giv-en and free, yeah. When you and I em-brace sur-ren - der,
Fmaj7
Dm7
G
D.S. al Coda
you and I choose to be-lieve, then you and I will see, you and I will see.
CODA
C
F
Yeah, we were meant to be,

Dm7
G
C
mmm.
You and I,
you and I,
F
Dm7
yeah,
yeah,
mmm,
G
C
F/C
and we were meant to be.
C
Csus2
3fr
C
F/C
C
C5
3fr

MOUNTAIN OF GOD

Words and Music by MAC POWELL
and BROWN BANNISTER

Bm
Em7
G
A(add4)
with me. Yes, You were there with me. Until You
with me. Yes, You are here with me. Well, I con-
C
G/B
A(add4)
o-pened up my eyes, I nev-er knew that I
fess, from time to time I lose my way, but You are
C
G/B
A(add4)
could-n't ev-er make it with-out You.
al-ways there to bring me back a-gain.
And e-ven though the
D5
5fr
Asus
jour-ney's long, and I know the road is hard, well, the One

Em7
G5
3fr
A5
5fr
who's gone be-fore me, He will help me car - ry on. And af - ter all that
D5
5fr
Asus
I've been through, well, now I re - al - ize the truth, that I must
Em7
1
G5
3fr
A5
5fr
go through the val - ley to stand up - on the moun - tain of God.
D5
5fr
2
G5
3fr
Asus
A
And up - on the moun - tain of God.

Fsus2
D5
Some-times I think of where it is I've come from,
Fsus2
D5
and the things I've left be-hind. But of all
Bm
E7/G♯
I've had, what I've pos-sessed, noth-ing can quite com-pare with what's in front
G5
A7sus
of me, with what's in front of me. Yeah, yeah.

N.C.
E5
E - ven though the jour - ney's long, and I know the
Bsus
F♯m
road is hard, yeah, the One who's gone be-fore me, He will help
A
B5
E5
me car - ry on. And af - ter all that I've been through, now I re - al -
Bsus
F♯m
ize the truth, that I must go through the val - ley to stand

A
B5
F♯m7
up-on the moun-tain. Yes, I must go through the val-ley to stand
A
B5
F♯m7
up-on the moun-tain. Yes, I must go through the val-ley to stand
A
Bsus
E5
up-on the moun - tain.
I thought that I was all a-lone,
Bsus
F♯m11
A(add2)
bro-ken and a-fraid, but You are here with me. Yes, You are here with me.
rit.

MY SAVIOR MY GOD

Words and Music by
AARON SHUST

A
I on - ly know at His right hand
stands One who is my
D
Sav - ior.
I take Him at His word and
deed.
bring
mf
Bm7
Christ died to save me, this I read,
my strength, my sol - ace from this spring
and in my heart I find a
that He who lives to be my
Asus
need
King
D
of Him to be my Sav - ior.
once died to be my Sav - ior.

G
That He would leave His place on high
and come for sin - ful men to ___
D
die.
You count it strange, so once did ___
Asus
I ___
be - fore I knew my
D
Sav - ior.
My Sav - ior loves, ___
f
Bm
___ my Sav - ior lives, ___
G
my Sav - ior's
D
al - ways there for
A
me. ___
My God He was, ___

Bm G D A
my God He is, my God is al - ways gon - na be. My Sav - ior loves,
Bm G D A
my Sav - ior lives, my Sav - ior's al - ways there for me. My God He was,
Bm G D
my God He is, my God is al - ways gon - na be.
Asus
1
2
Yes, liv - ing, dy - ing, let me

D
Bm7
mf
A
D
Bm7
Gsus2
mp
My Savior loves, my Savior lives, my Savior's
D
A/C♯
Bm7
Gsus2
always there for me. My God He was, my God He is, my God is

D
A/C♯
Bm7
al - ways gon - na be. My Sav - ior loves, my Sav - ior lives, my Sav - ior's
cresc. poco a poco
A/C♯
Gsus2
al - ways there for me. My God He was, my God He is, my God is
A
Bm
G
al - ways gon - na be. My Sav - ior loves, my Sav - ior lives, my Sav - ior's
f
D
A
Bm
G
al - ways there for me. My God He was, my God He is, my God is

D
A
Bm
al - ways gon - na be. My Sav - ior loves, my Sav - ior lives, my Sav - ior's
A/C♯
G
al - ways there for me. My God He was, my God He is, my God is
A
G
al - ways gon - na be. My Sav - ior lives, my Sav - ior loves, my Sav - ior lives,
dim. to end
Gsus2
my Sav - ior loves, my Sav - ior lives.

PRAISE YOU IN THIS STORM

Words and Music by MARK HALL
and BERNIE HERMS

*Recorded a half step higher.

F
C
Gm
and it's still rain - ing.
if I can't find You?
But as the thun - der rolls, I
B♭(add2)
3fr
Dm
C
bare - ly hear You whis - per through the rain,
"I'm with you."
And
Gm
B♭(add2)
3fr
as Your mer - cy falls,
I raise my hands and praise the God who gives
F
C
Dm
and takes a - way.
And I'll praise You in this storm,
f

B♭
F
and I will lift my hands, for You are who You are,
C
Dm
no mat-ter where I am. And ev-'ry tear I've cried
B♭
F
You hold in Your hand. You nev-er left my side.
C/E
Gm
B♭
And though my heart is torn, I will praise You in this storm.

F
1
Am
2
Am
Gm7
3fr
B♭
F
I lift my eyes un - to the hills.
Where does my help come _ from?
My help comes from the Lord, _ the
mf
Am
Gm7
3fr
Mak - er of Heav - en and Earth. _
I lift my eyes un - to the hills.
building
B♭
F
Where does my help come _ from?
My help comes from the Lord, _ the

Am
Gm7
3fr
Mak - er of Heav - en and Earth.
f
B♭
F
Am
Dm
B♭
And I'll praise You in this storm,
and I will lift my hands,
F
C
for You are who You are,
no mat - ter where I am.

Dm
Bb
And ev-'ry tear I've cried
You hold in Your hand.
F
C
You nev-er left my side.
And though my heart is torn,
Gm7
Bb
I will praise You in this storm.
F
Am
And though my heart is torn,

Gm
B♭
F
I praise You in this storm.
Am
Gm
B♭
F
Am
Gm
B♭
F
Am
Dm

REAL TO ME

Words and Music by JAY JOYCE,
NICHOLE NORDEMAN and JILL TOMALTY

Gmaj9
Bm7
Bm7/A
Gmaj9
Just an - oth - er hoop to jump through, an - oth - er mile of
Bm7
D6
Gsus2
Bm7
cov - ered ground.
Gmaj9
Bm7
Bm7/A
Gmaj9
I am wea - ry of the an - swers; more theo - ry and
Ev - 'ry scribe and ev - 'ry schol - ar, no win - ners in this
Bm7
D6
Gmaj9
cli - ché. They raise the let - ter of the
de - bate. Ev - 'ry - bod - y seems to

Bm7
Bm7/A
Gmaj9
Bm7
D6
law like a ban - ner till You're small and far a - way.
stand up tall - er when You're eas - y to ex - plain.
Em7
A
Em7
All the ques - tions in my head are from
I don't need to know what I don't know, just got -
A
F
C
my heart in - stead.
- ta let it go.
Be real to me now;
Gm7
B♭sus2
F
that's all I'm ask - ing.
Be real

1
C
Gm7
B♭sus2
to me now.
2
C
Gm7
B♭sus2
some - how, more than an - y - thing,
Dm
B♭sus2
Gmaj9
Bm7
D/F♯
more than an - y - thing.
G(add2)
Bm7
D/F♯
G(add2)
Bm7
D/F♯
G(add2)
Bm7
D6

Em7
Asus
A
Em7
So lay down the sword and put
Asus
A
Em7
a - way the doc - trine. Love a lit - tle more, love
C(add2)
N.C.
a lit - tle more, 'cause ev - 'ry - bod - y's bro - ken.
F
C
Gm7
Be real to me now; that's all

B♭sus2
F
C
I'm ask - ing.
Be real
some - how,
Gm7
1
B♭sus2
2
B♭sus2
more
than an - y - thing.
than an - y - thing,
Dm
B♭sus2
Dm
more
than an - y - thing.
Be real

B♭sus2
F
C
to me now.
Gm7
B♭(add2)
3fr
F
C
Gm7
B♭(add2)
3fr
Repeat and Fade
Optional Ending
F

SO LONG SELF

Words and Music by BART MILLARD, BARRY GRAUL,
JIM BRYSON, NATHAN COCHRAN,
MIKE SCHEUCHZER and ROBBY SHAFFER

A♭
4fr
Fm
Be - lieve it or not, but life is not,
And come to think of it, the blame
G♭
B♭m
A♭
4fr
ap - par - ent - ly, a - bout me an - y - ways. But I have met
for all of this sim - ply falls on me for want - ing some -
B♭m
G♭
the One who real - ly is wor - thy, so let me say:
- thing more in life than all of this. Oh, can't you see?
A♭
4fr
G♭
So long self; well, it's been fun, but I have found

D♭
A♭
somebody else. So long self; there's just no room
G♭
D♭
A♭
for two, so you are gonna have to move. So long self;
A♭maj7
E♭m7
D♭
don't take this wrong, but you are wrong for me. Farewell,
A♭
G♭
To Coda
oh well, goodbye, don't cry.

1
D♭
A♭
4fr
Oh, so long self.
B♭m
G♭
2
D♭
Oh, so long.
F♭
A♭
4fr
Don't feel so bad. (Don't
feel so bad.)
F♭
There'll be bet - ter days.

A♭
(There'll be bet - ter days.)
F♭
Don't
go a - way mad,
A♭
but by all means, just
F♭
go a - way,
G♭
go a - way.
A♭

G♭/B♭
6fr
G♭
A♭
4fr
B♭m
G♭
D.S. al Coda
CODA
D♭
A♭
4fr
Oh, so long self. Fare - well, good -
B♭m
G♭
A♭
4fr
bye. Oh, so long self. Fare -

B♭m
G♭
well, good - bye. Oh, so long self.
G♭
A♭
Fm
so long self. Fare - well, good -
B♭m
G♭
A♭
bye. Oh, so long self. Fare -
Fm
B♭m
G♭
Repeat and Fade
Optional Ending
A♭
well, good - bye. Oh, so long self.

STRONG TOWER

Words and Music by MARC BYRD, MARK LEE,
JON MICAH SUMRALL and AARON SPRINKLE

C♯m
4fr
B
Asus2
- ley and I'm tired and all a - lone, it seems like I've lost my
- ing and the thun - der's all I hear, You speak soft - ly to my
C♯m
4fr
F♯m7
E/G♯
way. I go run - ning to Your moun -
soul. Now I'm run - ning to Your moun -
Asus2
F♯m7
E/G♯
- tain, where Your mer - cy sets me
- tain, where Your mer - cy sets me
Asus2
E
free. You are my strong tow - er, a shel - ter o - ver me,
free.
f

C♯m7
4fr
Asus2
beau - ti - ful and might - y, ev - er - last - ing King.
B
E
You are my strong tow - er, a for - tress when I'm weak.
C♯m7
4fr
Asus2
Your name is true and ho - ly, and Your
B
C♯m7
4fr
A
1
2
face is all I seek.
And Your

B C♯m7 A B C♯m7 A
face is all I seek. Yeah, Your face is all I seek.
F♯m7 E/G♯ Asus2
I go run-ning to Your moun - tain,
F♯m7 E/G♯ Asus2
where Your mer - cy sets me free. You are my strong tow -
E C♯m7
- er, a shel - ter o - ver me, beau - ti - ful and might -
mf
f
4fr

Asusz2
- y, ev - er - last - ing King. You are my strong tow -
E
C♯m7
4fr
- er, a for - tress when I'm weak. Your name is true and ho -
1
2
Asus2
B
Asus2
- ly. You are my strong tow - - ly, and Your
B
C♯m7
4fr
A
B5
C♯5
4fr
A
face is all I seek.

WELCOME HOME
(You)

Words and Music by BRIAN LITTRELL
and DAN MUCKALA

B♭sus2
Gm7
Fa - ther said: You're nev - er far. I will be
F/B♭
Dm7
Gm7
where you are. And when you come to
B♭sus2
Me, I will o - pen My arms. Wel - come home,
F
C/E
B♭sus2
you. I know you by name. How do you do? I shine be-cause of

Dm7
Am7
you to - day. So come and sit down, tell me how you are. I know,
B♭sus2
To Coda
F
son, it's good just to see your face.
C/E
Dm7
B♭sus2
When I
F
C/E
Dm7
look at you hold - in' my heart, I will give to you all that I

B♭sus2
F
C/E
have. Son, I know there'll be times you will feel all a - lone. I will
Dm7
B♭sus2
Gm7
share with you the words my Fa - ther said: You're nev - er
F/B♭
Dm7
far. I will be where you are. And when you
Gm7
B♭sus2
come to Me you can bet I will o - pen My

D.S. al Coda
CODA
Gm7
F
C/E
Gm7
B♭sus2
F
C/E
arms. Wel - come home,
see your face.
So I'll be
wait - ing for that day,
just to feel Your warm em - brace.
Your love has shown I will nev - er be a - lone,
for
You will wel - come me home.

B♭/D
B♭
Dm7
I'll for - ev - er be, for You will
Am7
B♭sus2
C
Dm7
F
say to me, "Wel - come home,
C/E
B♭sus2
you. I know you by name. How do you do? I shine be-cause of
Dm7
you to - day. So come and sit down, tell me how you

Am7
B♭sus2
are. I know, son, it's good just to
Gm7
F
see your face." When I left home to
mp
C/E
Dm7
B♭sus2
be who I am, some peo - ple said, "No way."

WE ARE ONE TONIGHT

Words and Music by JONATHAN FOREMAN
and TIM FOREMAN

Em7
We built these cit - ies to stand
I'm no vic - tim; I've paid
Csus2
Em7
so tall. We've lost
these dues. I came
Csus2
our walls.
to lose.
D5
Em7
Csus2
I don't wan - na lose you com - ing down,
I don't wan - na fight a - bout it now,
with the whole

D5
Em7
world up - side down. I don't have a soul to trust in now,
Csus2
G5
with the whole world up - side down. We are one
D5
Em7
Csus2
to - night and we're sing - ing it out.
G5
D5
Em7
We are one to - night and we're

Csus2
G5
D
dream - ing out loud. Though the world is flawed,
Em7
Csus2
G5
these scars will heal. We are one
D5
Em7
Csus2
G5
to - night, to - night, to - night,
D5
Em7
1
Csus2
to - night.

2
Csus2
3fr
G5
3fr
To - night,
D5
5fr
Em7
Csus2
3fr
to - night.
D5
5fr
Em
Csus2
3fr
I don't wan - na lose the com - mon ground, with the whole
D5
5fr
Em
world up - side down. I don't wan - na fight a - bout it now,

Csus2
Cmaj7(no3rd)
in a world that's burn-ing out. Let's
G5
D5
Em7
slow the eve-ning down, slow it down, slow down.
Csus2
G5
D5
Em7
Please slow down, down, down. The stars
Csus2
G5
D5
are com-ing out. We are one.

Em7
Csus2
3fr
G5
3fr
We are one.
We are one.
D5
5fr
Em7
Csus2
3fr
We are one to - night.
G5
3fr
D5
5fr
Em7
We are one to - night and we're
Csus2
3fr
G5
3fr
D5
5fr
sing - ing it out. We are one to - night

Em7
Csus2
G5
and we're dream - ing out loud. Though the world
D/A
G/B
Csus2
is flawed, these scars will heal.
G5
D5
Em7
We are one to - night, to - night,
Repeat and Fade
Csus2
to - night.
Optional Ending
Csus2
G5
to - night.

WHAT IT MEANS

Words and Music by
JEREMY CAMP

*Recorded a half step lower.

Am9
5fr
G/B
A7/C♯
But You have shown so end - less - ly how Your love
C
Am
G/B
pours o - ver me. No pic - ture can re - cre - ate the beau -
D
G
- ty that I see. Show me what it means
Am7
G/B
to live my life a sac - ri - fice. If

Em7 D C
on - ly I would re - al - ize how much it took to
Em7 D C
pay the price, I know I'd al - ways give
G Am Em D
ev - 'ry - thing to You.
To Coda
G Am Em D Em
I want this world

D
A7/C♯
C
to al - ways see
Your per - fect maj - es - ty,
Em
D
A7/C♯
re - flect - ing from my life, this bril - liant po - et - ry.
C
Am9
5fr
G/B
Writ - ten all o - ver this place, the signs
A7/C♯
C
Am
of all cre - a - tion that You breathed. Words can't

G/B
D
D.S. al Coda
e - ven state how much You mean to me.
CODA
Em
D
E♭
3fr
I want to face my ver - y crime
G
E♭
3fr
of not giv - ing all of mine. But I can feel
D
the hope You bring to me.

G
Am7
Show me what it means to live my life a
mp
G/B
Em7
D
sac - ri - fice. If on - ly I would re - al - ize how
C
G
much it took to pay the price. Show me what it means
mf
Am7
G/B
to live my life a sac - ri - fice. If

Em7 D C
on - ly I would re - al - ize how much it took to
Em7 D C
pay the price, I know I'd al - ways give
G Am Em D
ev - 'ry - thing to You.
G Am Em D C(add2)

WHOLLY YOURS

Words and Music by
DAVID CROWDER

Dsus2
A
A/C♯
that is bright and clean. The an - to - nym of me,
Dsus2
A/C♯
D
You are di - vin - i - ty. But a cer - tain sign of
A
E/G♯
A/C♯
D
grace is this: From the bro - ken earth,
A
E/G♯
E
flow - ers come up, push - ing through the dirt. And You are ho -

D A E A/C♯
-ly, ho - ly, ho - ly. All heav - en cries, "Ho -
D A E D A
-ly, ho - ly God." Oh, You are ho - ly, ho - ly, ho -
E A/C♯ D A E
-ly. I want to be ho - ly like You are.
A Amaj7/C♯ Dsus2 A A/C♯
You are ev - 'ry - thing

Dsus2
A
A/C♯
that is bright and clean, and You're cov - er - ing
Dsus2
A/C♯
D
me with Your maj - es - ty. And the tru - est sign of
A
E/G♯
A/C♯
D
grace was this: From wound - ed hands re -
A
E/G♯
E
- demp - tion fell down, lib - er - at - ing man. And You are ho -

D A E A/C♯
-ly, ho - ly, ho - ly. All heav-en cries, "Ho -
D A E D A
-ly, ho - ly God." Oh, You are ho - ly, ho - ly, ho -
E A/C♯ D A E
-ly. I want to be ho - ly like You are.
G D
But the hard - er I try, the more clear - ly can I

A
E/G♯
feel the depth of our fall and the weight of it all.
D
A/C♯
And so this might could be the most im - pos - si - ble thing:
A
E/G♯
Dmaj7
A
Your grand-ness in me, mak - ing me clean. Glo - ry, hal -
E
Dmaj7
A
E
- le - lu - jah! Glo - ry, glo - ry, hal - le - lu - jah! You are ho -

D A E A/C♯
-ly, ho - ly, ho - ly. All heav - en cries, "Ho -
D A E D A
-ly, ho - ly God." Oh, You are ho - ly, ho - ly, ho -
E A/C♯ D A E
-ly. I want to be ho - ly, ho - ly, God. So,
D A E F♯m7
here I am, all of me, fi - nal - ly ev - 'ry - thing, whol -

D A E
- ly, whol - ly, whol - ly. I am whol -
D A E
- ly, whol - ly, whol - ly, I am whol -
D A E A Amaj7/C♯
- ly, whol - ly, whol - ly Yours.
Dsus2 A Amaj7/C♯ Dsus2
I am who - ly Yours.

A
Amaj7/C♯
Dmaj7
I am full _ of earth _ and dirt and You.
Dsus2/F♯
Here _ I am, _
D
Dmaj7
D6
Dsus2/F♯
ev - 'ry - thing. _
Asus/E
A/E
Repeat and Fade
Optional Ending

YOUR NAME

Words and Music by PAUL BALOCHE
and GLEN PACKLAM

*Recorded a half step lower.

G5 C5 Am7 Fsus2 G5 Am7
songs of praise that rise from earth to touch Your heart and
Fsus2 G C5 G Am7
glo - ri - fy Your name. Your name is a
C Fsus2 G Am7
strong and might - y tow - er. Your name is a
C Fsus2 G Am7
shel - ter like no oth - er. Your name, let the

C
Fsus2
C/E
Fsus2
To Coda
na - tions sing it loud - er, 'cause noth - ing has the pow - er to save
G
Csus2/E
Fsus2
G/B
Am7
but Your name.
Csus2/E
Fsus2
G/B
Am7
C/E
Fsus2
G5
3fr
C5
3fr
C/E
Fsus2
Je - sus, in Your name we pray, come and fill our

G5
C5
Am7
Fsus2
G
Am7
3fr
3fr
hearts to - day. Lord, give us strength to live for You and
F
G
C
D.S. al Coda
CODA
G
glo - ri - fy Your name. Your name
but Your name.
Am7
G6
Dsus(add2)
5fr
D
Am7
G6
Dsus(add2)
5fr

F G Am7 C/E Fsus2
'Cause Your name is a strong and might - y tow - er. Your name
mp
f sub.
G Am7 C Fsus2
is a shel - ter like no oth - er. Your name,
G Am7 C Fsus2
let the na - tions sing it loud - er, 'cause
C/E Fsus2 G
noth - ing has the pow - er to save. Your name

G
Am7
C
Fsus2
is a strong and might - y tow - er. Your name
G
Am7
C
Fsus2
is a shel - ter like no oth - er. Your name,
G
Am7
C
Fsus2
let the na - tions sing it loud - er, 'cause
C/E
Fsus2
G
noth - ing has the pow - er to save but Your name.

Csus2/E
Fsus2
G/B
Am7
Na na na na na na.
Na na na na na na.
Csus2/E
Fsus2
G/B
Am7
Na na na na na na.
Na na na na na na.
Csus2/E
Fsus2
G/B
Am7
mf
Csus2/E
Fsus2
G5
3fr
C5
3fr
rit.